I Manifested This Sh*t

*"For the
Kings & Queens
who want to
tap into
their elevation"*

Shamirah A. Briddle-Charriez

"Goddess Ifasade"

This book is dedicated to my ancestors who meant good and not evil. The kings, queens, warriors, gods, and goddesses. The ones who were cuffed and shackled in chains. Beaten and whipped to forget where they came from and their original African names. The ones that paved the way for me even in their darkest hours. The ones that sacrificed their lives to build me. The ones that prayed and cried all night long for the next generations to prosper and persevere.

God, I thank you for my mother and dedicate this book to her, Corrine D. Briddle, she put her life on the line to bring me into this world, and you kept us both. You continue to inspire me, everything I do is for you.

I dedicate this book to my great-grandparents, grandparents, mom, father, brother, son, husband, dog Neffy, aunts, uncles, god-parents, god-sisters, god-brothers, god-children and my Sista friends.

To my husband Chris, you are the beam that our light needed. Thankyou for seeing me and loving me how you do.

To my son Zion, you are my proof that God performs miracles. I love you with every cell in me. Continue the path created for you and remember to always stay in God's face. Always remain uniquely you and hear my words of wisdom in your ears. Remember your name!

To my best friend Tabitha Stokes who passed away in 2015, I know you are screaming "That's MY BFF" in heaven.

All of you inspire me to always push and keep my crown on.

A special thanks to Queen Afua, Hadiiya Barbel, Iya Funlayo E. Wood, PhD, Iya Rosa, Baba Nelson, and Araba Chief Adedayo Ologundudu. I am here because of the wisdom you have imparted, the grace you have extended, and the safe space you have allowed for me to be open, honest and vulnerable.

A special dedication to my first cousin Andrew (Trub) Johnson Jr.,
God called you right before the announcement of this birth. You will never be forgotten. You have your wings now...."What a might God we serve". Continue to Sleep in Peace 12/18/22.
YOU ARE HEALED!

I want to give thanks and praise to God (Olodumare) and all my Orishas and ancestors of good character that came before me. Calling on them to birth this baby led me into the right hands. I come from women who had proverbs and psalms in their mouth.

A Simple Guide:

You can re-write the affirmations as they are, or you can use the lines to say the affirmations your way.

The pictures on the following pages are adrinka symbols that aid in manifestation.

Gye Nyame (je N-yah-mee) - except God, only God. "No one lives who saw its beginning and no one will live to see its end, Except God".

Asase Ye Duru (Ah-sah-se yeah doo-rooo) - representation of providence and the divinity of Mother Earth.

Duafe (doo-ah-phe) - representation of feminine consideration or good feminine qualities: patience, prudence, fondness, love and care.

Dwennimmen (djwin-knee-mann)- representation of strength in mind, body and soul, humility, wisdom and learning.

Eban (eh-ban) - representation of safety, security and love.

"No one is going to bother to put you down, if you are not a threat to them"-Cisely Tyson

"I MANIFESTED THIS SHIT"

For the Kings & Queens who want to tap into their elevation!

I'm no longer tucked in chapters with people who don't match my vibe. I had to remove myself from tables that served poison, from people I made priorities when they were options. I had to remember my worth. That I am the shit and I have the strength, courage, wisdom, and power to elevate.

I was spiritually pregnant and almost aborted what was inside of me every single time. I had to lean not on my own understanding and trust more in my higher power. When I began to stay in God's face and eliminate outside distractions, my vision became so much clearer. I kept hearing my ancestors say, "Don't let the gifts inside of you die".

In a world where we depend on human beings and material things to save us, I realized that what I really needed was inside of me all along, THE ABILITY TO MANIFEST"! This is the manifestation that confirmed the awakening of my spirit.

This book will give you the peace that you cannot buy, trade, sell nor tarnish. If you allow it, it will take you from pieces to having peace. It will give you a breakthrough and not a breakdown. It will give you power over the enemy and anything blocking your path. It truly set me free. I am healed because of my vision to create this book.

Before you turn to the next page. I invite you to connect with your higher power and inner self. Position yourself in a place where peace resides or create it. Speak to your higher power. Connect with your ancestors of good character. Ask for their assistance in this manifestation. Stay away from envy, malice, and jealousy, and follow your intuition. Remain in good character, don't live in anyone else's storm, and prepare for the elevation.

When you're reading this, you must speak and write with umph, meaning, conviction, belief, faith, and like grandma got a switch from the tree for that ass. Tap into warrior mode. Let the surgery, birthing, and healing take place. Allow the pages to flow, your writing utensil to dance, your mind to be free and focused, and don't forget to allow the universe to work. Speak those things as though they are! Get ready to give birth!

DAY OF THE WEEK: M ☐ T ☐ W ☐ TH ☐ F ☐ S ☐ S ☐

DATE _____   TIME _____

WHERE AM I NOW: HOME ☐   WORK ☐   OTHER _____

I AM MANIFESTING GREATNESS! EVEN BEFORE I WAS FORMED IN MY MOTHER'S WOMB, GOD ALREADY KNEW WHO I WAS AND WHAT I WAS GOING TO COME HERE TO DO.

I am manifesting greatness.... (repeat and write)

_____

_____

_____

_____

_____

_____

_____

_____

_____

_____

Manifestation is the power you have within. It is the ability to tap into your faith and discernment.

I MANIFESTED THIS SH*T

_____

_____

_____

_____

_____

_____

_____

_____

_____

_____

_____

_____

_____

_____

Manifestation is the power you have within. It is the ability to tap into your faith and discernment.

I MANIFESTED THIS SH*T

_____

_____

_____

_____

_____

_____

_____

_____

_____

_____

_____

_____

_____

Manifestation is the power you have within. It is the ability to tap into your faith and discernment.

I MANIFESTED THIS SH*T

Manifestation is the power you have within. It is the ability to tap into your faith and discernment.

DAY OF THE WEEK: M ☐ T ☐ W ☐ TH ☐ F ☐ S ☐ S ☐

DATE _____   TIME _____

WHERE AM I NOW: HOME ☐   WORK ☐   OTHER _____

WHEN THE UNIVERSE AND MY DIVINE ENERGY CONSECRATE TOGETHER, MANIFESTATION IS BIRTHED.

I am birthing_____.... (repeat and write)

_____

_____

_____

_____

_____

_____

_____

_____

_____

_____

Manifestation is the power you have within. It is the ability to tap into your faith and discernment.

I MANIFESTED THIS SH*T

Manifestation is the power you have within. It is the ability to tap into your faith and discernment.

I MANIFESTED THIS SH*T

_____

_____

_____

_____

_____

_____

_____

_____

_____

_____

_____

_____

Manifestation is the power you have within. It is the ability to tap into your faith and discernment.

I MANIFESTED THIS SH*T

_____

_____

_____

_____

_____

_____

_____

_____

_____

_____

_____

_____

_____

_____

Manifestation is the power you have within. It is the ability to tap into your faith and discernment.

DAY OF THE WEEK: M ☐ T ☐ W ☐ TH ☐ F ☐ S ☐ S ☐

DATE _____   TIME _____

WHERE AM I NOW: HOME ☐   WORK ☐   OTHER _____

MY HOUSING SITUATION WASN'T ALWAYS THE BEST AND AS A CHILD TO ME IT WAS HOME, MY SAFE SPACE. ENLARGE MY TERRITORY FOR GENERATIONAL WEALTH TO IMPROVE THE LIFE-CYCLE PATTERN OF HOME OWNERSHIP.

I am a homeowner.... (repeat and write)

_____

_____

_____

_____

_____

_____

_____

_____

_____

_____

Manifestation is the power you have within. It is the ability to tap into your faith and discernment.

I MANIFESTED THIS SH*T

Manifestation is the power you have within. It is the ability to tap into your faith and discernment.

I MANIFESTED THIS SH*T

_____

_____

_____

_____

_____

_____

_____

_____

_____

_____

_____

_____

_____

Manifestation is the power you have within. It is the ability to tap into your faith and discernment.

I MANIFESTED THIS SH*T

Manifestation is the power you have within. It is the ability to tap into your faith and discernment.

DAY OF THE WEEK: M ☐ T ☐ W ☐ TH ☐ F ☐ S ☐ S ☐

DATE _____   TIME _____

WHERE AM I NOW: HOME ☐   WORK ☐   OTHER _____

I WILL NOT DOWNPLAY MY UNIQUE SELF TO APPEASE OTHERS. I LOOK GOOD, I FEEL GOOD, I AM NOT LIKE ANYONE ELSE AND MOST OF ALL, I AM BLESSED!

I am blessed.... (repeat and write)

_____

_____

_____

_____

_____

_____

_____

_____

_____

_____

Manifestation is the power you have within. It is the ability to tap into your faith and discernment.

I MANIFESTED THIS SH*T

Manifestation is the power you have within. It is the ability to tap into your faith and discernment.

I MANIFESTED THIS SH*T

Manifestation is the power you have within. It is the ability to tap into your faith and discernment.

I MANIFESTED THIS SH*T

_____

_____

_____

_____

_____

_____

_____

_____

_____

_____

_____

_____

_____

_____

Manifestation is the power you have within. It is the ability to tap into your faith and discernment.

DAY OF THE WEEK: M ☐ T ☐ W ☐ TH ☐ F ☐ S ☐ S ☐

DATE _____   TIME _____

WHERE AM I NOW: HOME ☐   WORK ☐   OTHER _____

MY GRANDCHILDREN WILL KNOW THAT I WAS HERE, AND I DID THIS FOR THEM.

I am manifesting generational wealth.... (repeat and write)

_____

_____

_____

_____

_____

_____

_____

_____

_____

_____

Manifestation is the power you have within. It is the ability to tap into your faith and discernment.

I MANIFESTED THIS SH*T

Manifestation is the power you have within. It is the ability to tap into your faith and discernment.

I MANIFESTED THIS SH*T

_____

_____

_____

_____

_____

_____

_____

_____

_____

_____

_____

_____

_____

Manifestation is the power you have within. It is the ability to tap into your faith and discernment.

I MANIFESTED THIS SH*T

_____

_____

_____

_____

_____

_____

_____

_____

_____

_____

_____

_____

_____

Manifestation is the power you have within. It is the ability to tap into your faith and discernment.

DAY OF THE WEEK: M ☐ T ☐ W ☐ TH ☐ F ☐ S ☐ S ☐

DATE _____   TIME _____

WHERE AM I NOW: HOME ☐ WORK ☐ OTHER _____

EVERY ENERGY DOESN'T DESERVE YOUR PRESENCE – GET UP!

I am protecting my peace.... (repeat and write)

_____
_____
_____
_____
_____
_____
_____
_____
_____
_____

Manifestation is the power you have within. It is the ability to tap into your faith and discernment.

I MANIFESTED THIS SH*T

_____

_____

_____

_____

_____

_____

_____

_____

_____

_____

_____

_____

_____

Manifestation is the power you have within. It is the ability to tap into your faith and discernment.

I MANIFESTED THIS SH*T

_____

_____

_____

_____

_____

_____

_____

_____

_____

_____

_____

_____

_____

Manifestation is the power you have within. It is the ability to tap into your faith and discernment.

*I MANIFESTED THIS SH*T*

_____

_____

_____

_____

_____

_____

_____

_____

_____

_____

_____

_____

_____

Manifestation is the power you have within. It is the ability to tap into your faith and discernment.

DAY OF THE WEEK: M ☐ T ☐ W ☐ TH ☐ F ☐ S ☐ S ☐

DATE _____   TIME _____

WHERE AM I NOW: HOME ☐   WORK ☐   OTHER _____

THERE ARE MOMENTS WHEN I DON'T KNOW WHAT TO DO, BUT THEN A SPIRITED VOICE FILLS MY SOUL.

I am heavenly guided.... (repeat and write)

_____

_____

_____

_____

_____

_____

_____

_____

_____

_____

Manifestation is the power you have within. It is the ability to tap into your faith and discernment.

I MANIFESTED THIS SH*T

_____

_____

_____

_____

_____

_____

_____

_____

_____

_____

_____

_____

_____

Manifestation is the power you have within. It is the ability to tap into your faith and discernment.

I MANIFESTED THIS SH*T

_____

_____

_____

_____

_____

_____

_____

_____

_____

_____

_____

_____

_____

Manifestation is the power you have within. It is the ability to tap into your faith and discernment.

I MANIFESTED THIS SH*T

_____

_____

_____

_____

_____

_____

_____

_____

_____

_____

_____

_____

_____

_____

Manifestation is the power you have within. It is the ability to tap into your faith and discernment.

DAY OF THE WEEK: M ☐ T ☐ W ☐ TH ☐ F ☐ S ☐ S ☐

DATE _____   TIME _____

WHERE AM I NOW: HOME ☐   WORK ☐   OTHER _____

I NEED A FINANCIAL BLESSING. I SPEAK WITH AN ATTITUDE OF GRATITUDE FOR THE MONEY THAT IS COMING MY WAY.

I am manifesting a financial blessing.... (repeat and write)

_____

_____

_____

_____

_____

_____

_____

_____

_____

_____

Manifestation is the power you have within. It is the ability to tap into your faith and discernment.

I MANIFESTED THIS SH*T

_____

_____

_____

_____

_____

_____

_____

_____

_____

_____

_____

_____

Manifestation is the power you have within. It is the ability to tap into your faith and discernment.

I MANIFESTED THIS SH*T

_____

_____

_____

_____

_____

_____

_____

_____

_____

_____

_____

_____

Manifestation is the power you have within. It is the ability to tap into your faith and discernment.

I MANIFESTED THIS SH*T

Manifestation is the power you have within. It is the ability to tap into your faith and discernment.

DAY OF THE WEEK: M ☐ T ☐ W ☐ TH ☐ F ☐ S ☐ S ☐

DATE _____   TIME _____

WHERE AM I NOW: HOME ☐   WORK ☐   OTHER _____

I WILL HAVE PEACE AND VICTORY WITH EVERY DIFFICULT CONVERSATION I MUST HAVE.

My mind is clear and my words provide clarity.... (repeat and write)

_____

_____

_____

_____

_____

_____

_____

_____

_____

_____

Manifestation is the power you have within. It is the ability to tap into your faith and discernment.

I MANIFESTED THIS SH*T

_____

_____

_____

_____

_____

_____

_____

_____

_____

_____

_____

_____

_____

Manifestation is the power you have within. It is the ability to tap into your faith and discernment.

I MANIFESTED THIS SH*T

_____

_____

_____

_____

_____

_____

_____

_____

_____

_____

_____

_____

Manifestation is the power you have within. It is the ability to tap into your faith and discernment.

I MANIFESTED THIS SH*T

Manifestation is the power you have within. It is the ability to tap into your faith and discernment.

DAY OF THE WEEK: M ☐ T ☐ W ☐ TH ☐ F ☐ S ☐ S ☐

DATE _____   TIME _____

WHERE AM I NOW: HOME ☐   WORK ☐   OTHER _____

MY ANCESTORS CAME A LONG WAY AND SO WILL I.

I am constantly breaking chains, I am the chosen one.... (repeat and write)

_____

_____

_____

_____

_____

_____

_____

_____

_____

_____

Manifestation is the power you have within. It is the ability to tap into your faith and discernment.

I MANIFESTED THIS SH*T

_____

_____

_____

_____

_____

_____

_____

_____

_____

_____

_____

_____

_____

_____

Manifestation is the power you have within. It is the ability to tap into your faith and discernment.

I MANIFESTED THIS SH*T

_____

_____

_____

_____

_____

_____

_____

_____

_____

_____

_____

_____

_____

_____

Manifestation is the power you have within. It is the ability to tap into your faith and discernment.

I MANIFESTED THIS SH*T

_____

_____

_____

_____

_____

_____

_____

_____

_____

_____

_____

_____

_____

_____

Manifestation is the power you have within. It is the ability to tap into your faith and discernment.

DAY OF THE WEEK: M ☐ T ☐ W ☐ TH ☐ F ☐ S ☐ S ☐

DATE _____   TIME _____

WHERE AM I NOW: HOME ☐   WORK ☐   OTHER _____

WHEW, I AM BEING TESTED AND TRIED, LITTLE DO THEY KNOW THE SPIRIT OF MY ANCESTORS ARE PUSHING ME THROUGH.

I am manifesting victory over the situation.... (repeat and write)

_____

_____

_____

_____

_____

_____

_____

_____

_____

_____

Manifestation is the power you have within. It is the ability to tap into your faith and discernment.

I MANIFESTED THIS SH*T

_____

_____

_____

_____

_____

_____

_____

_____

_____

_____

_____

_____

_____

Manifestation is the power you have within. It is the ability to tap into your faith and discernment.

I MANIFESTED THIS SH*T

_____

_____

_____

_____

_____

_____

_____

_____

_____

_____

_____

_____

Manifestation is the power you have within. It is the ability to tap into your faith and discernment.

I MANIFESTED THIS SH*T

_____

_____

_____

_____

_____

_____

_____

_____

_____

_____

_____

_____

_____

Manifestation is the power you have within. It is the ability to tap into your faith and discernment.

DAY OF THE WEEK: M ☐ T ☐ W ☐ TH ☐ F ☐ S ☐ S ☐

DATE _____   TIME _____

WHERE AM I NOW: HOME ☐   WORK ☐   OTHER _____

THIS SPIRITUAL WALK IS NOT EASY. I WILL STAY GROUNDED AND CONTINUE TO WALK AND EMBRACE THE PATH DESTINED FOR ME.

I am manifesting a path of divine connections.... (repeat and write)

_____

_____

_____

_____

_____

_____

_____

_____

_____

_____

_____

Manifestation is the power you have within. It is the ability to tap into your faith and discernment.

I MANIFESTED THIS SH*T

_____

_____

_____

_____

_____

_____

_____

_____

_____

_____

_____

_____

_____

_____

Manifestation is the power you have within. It is the ability to tap into your faith and discernment.

I MANIFESTED THIS SH*T

Manifestation is the power you have within. It is the ability to tap into your faith and discernment.

I MANIFESTED THIS SH*T

_____

_____

_____

_____

_____

_____

_____

_____

_____

_____

_____

_____

_____

_____

Manifestation is the power you have within. It is the ability to tap into your faith and discernment.

DAY OF THE WEEK: M ☐ T ☐ W ☐ TH ☐ F ☐ S ☐ S ☐

DATE _____   TIME _____

WHERE AM I NOW: HOME ☐   WORK ☐   OTHER _____

MAKE UP YOUR MIND OF WHO YOU DESIRE TO BE AND LET IT REFLECT YOUR CHARACTER.

I will stay in good character.... (repeat and write)

_____

_____

_____

_____

_____

_____

_____

_____

_____

_____

Manifestation is the power you have within. It is the ability to tap into your faith and discernment.

I MANIFESTED THIS SH*T

Manifestation is the power you have within. It is the ability to tap into your faith and discernment.

I MANIFESTED THIS SH*T

Manifestation is the power you have within. It is the ability to tap into your faith and discernment.

I MANIFESTED THIS SH*T

Manifestation is the power you have within. It is the ability to tap into your faith and discernment.

DAY OF THE WEEK: M ☐   T ☐   W ☐   TH ☐   F ☐   S ☐   S ☐

DATE _____   TIME _____

WHERE AM I NOW: HOME ☐   WORK ☐   OTHER _____

EVERYBODY'S SPIRITUAL PATH IS NOT THE SAME. WHAT'S FOR YOU IS FOR YOU.

I am spiritually guided to do great things.... (repeat and write)

_____

_____

_____

_____

_____

_____

_____

_____

_____

_____

_____

Manifestation is the power you have within. It is the ability to tap into your faith and discernment.

I MANIFESTED THIS SH*T

Manifestation is the power you have within. It is the ability to tap into your faith and discernment.

I MANIFESTED THIS SH*T

Manifestation is the power you have within. It is the ability to tap into your faith and discernment.

I MANIFESTED THIS SH*T

Manifestation is the power you have within. It is the ability to tap into your faith and discernment.

DAY OF THE WEEK: M ☐ T ☐ W ☐ TH ☐ F ☐ S ☐ S ☐

DATE _____   TIME _____

WHERE AM I NOW: HOME ☐   WORK ☐   OTHER _____

I NO LONGER ALLOW ANYONE TO TAINT MY VISION, LEACH ON ME NOR BECOME A SPIRIT SUCKER IN MY LIFE, THOSE DAYS ARE OVER.

I remove myself from toxic relationships and birth healthy ones.... (repeat and write)

_____

_____

_____

_____

_____

_____

_____

_____

_____

_____

_____

Manifestation is the power you have within. It is the ability to tap into your faith and discernment.

I MANIFESTED THIS SH*T

_____

_____

_____

_____

_____

_____

_____

_____

_____

_____

_____

_____

_____

_____

Manifestation is the power you have within. It is the ability to tap into your faith and discernment.

I MANIFESTED THIS SH*T

Manifestation is the power you have within. It is the ability to tap into your faith and discernment.

I MANIFESTED THIS SH*T

Manifestation is the power you have within. It is the ability to tap into your faith and discernment.

DAY OF THE WEEK: M ☐ T ☐ W ☐ TH ☐ F ☐ S ☐ S ☐

DATE _____   TIME _____

WHERE AM I NOW: HOME ☐   WORK ☐   OTHER _____

AND IT IS WELL WITH MY SOUL, I AM OPEN AND READY TO RECEIVE AND BE A PARTNER IN A HEALTHY RELATIONSHIP.

I will not bring the residue of my past relationships into my new one.... (repeat and write)

_____

_____

_____

_____

_____

_____

_____

_____

_____

_____

Manifestation is the power you have within. It is the ability to tap into your faith and discernment.

I MANIFESTED THIS SH*T

Manifestation is the power you have within. It is the ability to tap into your faith and discernment.

I MANIFESTED THIS SH*T

Manifestation is the power you have within. It is the ability to tap into your faith and discernment.

I MANIFESTED THIS SH*T

Manifestation is the power you have within. It is the ability to tap into your faith and discernment.

DAY OF THE WEEK: M ☐ T ☐ W ☐ TH ☐ F ☐ S ☐ S ☐

DATE _____   TIME _____

WHERE AM I NOW: HOME ☐   WORK ☐   OTHER _____

THEY SAY THAT "LOVE IS WHAT LOVE DOES". SO LET ME JUST GO AHEAD AND LOVE ON MYSELF.

I am manifesting the love I wish to receive for myself.... (repeat and write)

_____

_____

_____

_____

_____

_____

_____

_____

_____

_____

_____

Manifestation is the power you have within. It is the ability to tap into your faith and discernment.

_____

_____

_____

_____

_____

_____

_____

_____

_____

_____

_____

_____

_____

_____

Manifestation is the power you have within. It is the ability to tap into your faith and discernment.

I MANIFESTED THIS SH*T

_____

_____

_____

_____

_____

_____

_____

_____

_____

_____

_____

_____

Manifestation is the power you have within. It is the ability to tap into your faith and discernment.

I MANIFESTED THIS SH*T

Manifestation is the power you have within. It is the ability to tap into your faith and discernment.

DAY OF THE WEEK: M ☐   T ☐   W ☐   TH ☐   F ☐   S ☐   S ☐

DATE _____   TIME _____

WHERE AM I NOW: HOME ☐   WORK ☐   OTHER _____

SISTERHOOD IS A TERM THAT HAS BEEN THROWN AROUND LATELY. BE SURE IT MATCHES UP WITH YOUR CHARACTER AND WALK.

I reflect the type of sister I would want in my life…. (repeat and write)

_____

_____

_____

_____

_____

_____

_____

_____

_____

_____

Manifestation is the power you have within. It is the ability to tap into your faith and discernment.

I MANIFESTED THIS SH*T

_____

_____

_____

_____

_____

_____

_____

_____

_____

_____

_____

_____

Manifestation is the power you have within. It is the ability to tap into your faith and discernment.

I MANIFESTED THIS SH*T

Manifestation is the power you have within. It is the ability to tap into your faith and discernment.

I MANIFESTED THIS SH*T

_____

_____

_____

_____

_____

_____

_____

_____

_____

_____

_____

_____

_____

Manifestation is the power you have within. It is the ability to tap into your faith and discernment.

DAY OF THE WEEK: M ☐   T ☐   W ☐ TH ☐   F ☐   S ☐   S ☐

DATE _____   TIME _____

WHERE AM I NOW: HOME ☐   WORK ☐   OTHER _____

BROTHERHOOD IS OFTEN MISUNDERSTOOD AND UNDERRATED. EVERY BOY/MAN NEEDS TO SEE A BROTHER THAT IS A STRONG, SPIRITED, POSITIVE ROLE MODEL.

What I want and need for my brother, is what I want and need for myself.... (repeat and write)

_____

_____

_____

_____

_____

_____

_____

_____

_____

_____

Manifestation is the power you have within. It is the ability to tap into your faith and discernment.

I MANIFESTED THIS SH*T

Manifestation is the power you have within. It is the ability to tap into your faith and discernment.

I MANIFESTED THIS SH*T

Manifestation is the power you have within. It is the ability to tap into your faith and discernment.

I MANIFESTED THIS SH*T

Manifestation is the power you have within. It is the ability to tap into your faith and discernment.

DAY OF THE WEEK: M ☐   T ☐   W ☐ TH ☐   F ☐   S ☐   S ☐

DATE _____   TIME _____

WHERE AM I NOW: HOME ☐   WORK ☐   OTHER _____

I AM GRATEFUL FOR MY STREAM OF INCOME, BUT I CANNOT STAY HERE. I AM READY FOR THE NEXT LEVEL.

I am manifesting a new career.... (repeat and write)

_____

_____

_____

_____

_____

_____

_____

_____

_____

_____

Manifestation is the power you have within. It is the ability to tap into your faith and discernment.

I MANIFESTED THIS SH*T

_____

_____

_____

_____

_____

_____

_____

_____

_____

_____

_____

_____

_____

Manifestation is the power you have within. It is the ability to tap into your faith and discernment.

I MANIFESTED THIS SH*T

_____

_____

_____

_____

_____

_____

_____

_____

_____

_____

_____

_____

_____

Manifestation is the power you have within. It is the ability to tap into your faith and discernment.

I MANIFESTED THIS SH*T

Manifestation is the power you have within. It is the ability to tap into your faith and discernment.

DAY OF THE WEEK: M ☐   T ☐   W ☐ TH ☐   F ☐   S ☐   S ☐

DATE _____   TIME _____

WHERE AM I NOW: HOME ☐   WORK ☐   OTHER _____

THE GOD/GODDESS IN ME IS RISING. THERE IS NO ROOM FOR STAGNATION. I MUST ELEVATE DAILY LIKE THE SUN.

I am constantly evolving.... (repeat and write)

_____

_____

_____

_____

_____

_____

_____

_____

_____

_____

Manifestation is the power you have within. It is the ability to tap into your faith and discernment.

I MANIFESTED THIS SH*T

Manifestation is the power you have within. It is the ability to tap into your faith and discernment.

I MANIFESTED THIS SH*T

_____

_____

_____

_____

_____

_____

_____

_____

_____

_____

_____

_____

_____

Manifestation is the power you have within. It is the ability to tap into your faith and discernment.

I MANIFESTED THIS SH*T

Manifestation is the power you have within. It is the ability to tap into your faith and discernment.

DAY OF THE WEEK: M ☐ T ☐ W ☐ TH ☐ F ☐ S ☐ S ☐

DATE _____   TIME _____

WHERE AM I NOW: HOME ☐   WORK ☐   OTHER _____

MY SUPERPOWERS ARE NOTHING TO BE PLAYED WITH. I PRAYED AND COMMANDED MANIFESTATIONS TO HAPPEN AND NOW HERE I AM.

My manifestations have power.... (repeat and write)

_____

_____

_____

_____

_____

_____

_____

_____

_____

_____

_____

Manifestation is the power you have within. It is the ability to tap into your faith and discernment.

I MANIFESTED THIS SH*T

Manifestation is the power you have within. It is the ability to tap into your faith and discernment.

I MANIFESTED THIS SH*T

_____

_____

_____

_____

_____

_____

_____

_____

_____

_____

_____

_____

_____

Manifestation is the power you have within. It is the ability to tap into your faith and discernment.

I MANIFESTED THIS SH*T

_____

_____

_____

_____

_____

_____

_____

_____

_____

_____

_____

_____

Manifestation is the power you have within. It is the ability to tap into your faith and discernment.

DAY OF THE WEEK: M ☐ T ☐ W ☐ TH ☐ F ☐ S ☐ S ☐

DATE _____   TIME _____

WHERE AM I NOW: HOME ☐   WORK ☐   OTHER _____

SOMETIMES MY MIND IS ALL OVER THE PLACE ALONG WITH MY BODY AND SPIRIT. I WON'T ALLOW THE ISSUES OF OTHERS TO TILT MY CROWN. I AM IN THE HEALING ROOM AND MY CROWN IS ON.

I am manifesting being healthy in mind, body and spirit.... (repeat and write)

_____

_____

_____

_____

_____

_____

_____

_____

_____

_____

_____

Manifestation is the power you have within. It is the ability to tap into your faith and discernment.

I MANIFESTED THIS SH*T

_____

_____

_____

_____

_____

_____

_____

_____

_____

_____

_____

_____

_____

Manifestation is the power you have within. It is the ability to tap into your faith and discernment.

I MANIFESTED THIS SH*T

Manifestation is the power you have within. It is the ability to tap into your faith and discernment.

I MANIFESTED THIS SH*T

Manifestation is the power you have within. It is the ability to tap into your faith and discernment.

DAY OF THE WEEK: M ☐ T ☐ W ☐ TH ☐ F ☐ S ☐ S ☐

DATE _____   TIME _____

WHERE AM I NOW: HOME ☐   WORK ☐   OTHER _____

THERE ARE TIMES WHEN FEAR GETS IN THE WAY. NO LONGER WILL I ALLOW MY FEARS TO OVERSHADOW MY CONFIDENCE.

I am an overcomer, I will not self-sabotage myself.... (repeat and write)

_____

_____

_____

_____

_____

_____

_____

_____

_____

_____

_____

Manifestation is the power you have within. It is the ability to tap into your faith and discernment.

I MANIFESTED THIS SH*T

Manifestation is the power you have within. It is the ability to tap into your faith and discernment.

I MANIFESTED THIS SH*T

Manifestation is the power you have within. It is the ability to tap into your faith and discernment.

I MANIFESTED THIS SH*T

_____

_____

_____

_____

_____

_____

_____

_____

_____

_____

_____

_____

_____

_____

Manifestation is the power you have within. It is the ability to tap into your faith and discernment.

DAY OF THE WEEK: M ☐ T ☐ W ☐ TH ☐ F ☐ S ☐ S ☐

DATE _____   TIME _____

WHERE AM I NOW: HOME ☐   WORK ☐   OTHER _____

THE PAIN I FELT AND CAUSED LED ME TO A ROAD OF ROLLERCOASTER RIDES. I GOT OFF AND KNEW THAT THE ALMIGHTY HAS GIVEN ME YET, ANOTHER CHANCE.

I am manifesting turning my pain into redemption.... (repeat and write)

_____

_____

_____

_____

_____

_____

_____

_____

_____

_____

_____

Manifestation is the power you have within. It is the ability to tap into your faith and discernment.

I MANIFESTED THIS SH*T

_____

_____

_____

_____

_____

_____

_____

_____

_____

_____

_____

_____

_____

Manifestation is the power you have within. It is the ability to tap into your faith and discernment.

I MANIFESTED THIS SH*T

_____

_____

_____

_____

_____

_____

_____

_____

_____

_____

_____

_____

_____

Manifestation is the power you have within. It is the ability to tap into your faith and discernment.

I MANIFESTED THIS SH*T

_____

_____

_____

_____

_____

_____

_____

_____

_____

_____

_____

_____

_____

Manifestation is the power you have within. It is the ability to tap into your faith and discernment.

DAY OF THE WEEK: M ☐ T ☐ W ☐ TH ☐ F ☐ S ☐ S ☐

DATE _____   TIME _____

WHERE AM I NOW: HOME ☐   WORK ☐   OTHER _____

FORGETTING TO SAY OR FALLING ASLEEP BEFORE SAYING MY PRAYERS ALWAYS MAKES ME FEEL LIKE I DISAPPOINTED GOD. THEN I AM REMINDED THAT GOD KNOWS MY THOUGHTS AND MY HEART.

I am manifesting a daily prayer life.... (repeat and write)

_____

_____

_____

_____

_____

_____

_____

_____

_____

_____

Manifestation is the power you have within. It is the ability to tap into your faith and discernment.

I MANIFESTED THIS SH*T

_____

_____

_____

_____

_____

_____

_____

_____

_____

_____

_____

_____

Manifestation is the power you have within. It is the ability to tap into your faith and discernment.

I MANIFESTED THIS SH*T

_____

_____

_____

_____

_____

_____

_____

_____

_____

_____

_____

_____

_____

Manifestation is the power you have within. It is the ability to tap into your faith and discernment.

I MANIFESTED THIS SH*T

_____

_____

_____

_____

_____

_____

_____

_____

_____

_____

_____

_____

_____

Manifestation is the power you have within. It is the ability to tap into your faith and discernment.

DAY OF THE WEEK: M ☐ T ☐ W ☐ TH ☐ F ☐ S ☐ S ☐

DATE _____   TIME _____

WHERE AM I NOW: HOME ☐ WORK ☐ OTHER _____

IN EVERY SITUATION, PEOPLE WILL ALWAYS REMEMBER YOU FOR HOW YOU RESPONDED TO A SITUATION.

I will transmit positive energy everywhere I go.... (repeat and write)

_____

_____

_____

_____

_____

_____

_____

_____

_____

_____

Manifestation is the power you have within. It is the ability to tap into your faith and discernment.

I MANIFESTED THIS SH*T

Manifestation is the power you have within. It is the ability to tap into your faith and discernment.

I MANIFESTED THIS SH*T

Manifestation is the power you have within. It is the ability to tap into your faith and discernment.

I MANIFESTED THIS SH*T

_____

_____

_____

_____

_____

_____

_____

_____

_____

_____

_____

_____

_____

Manifestation is the power you have within. It is the ability to tap into your faith and discernment.

DAY OF THE WEEK: M ☐ T ☐ W ☐ TH ☐ F ☐ S ☐ S ☐

DATE _____   TIME _____

WHERE AM I NOW: HOME ☐   WORK ☐   OTHER _____

WHEN RETROGRADE COMES, I AM PREPARED FOR THE STORM COMING MY WAY. I TACKLE IT HEAD ON IN CONFIDENCE THAT A RAINBOW IS COMING.

Retrograde does not control me, I control it.... (repeat and write)

_____

_____

_____

_____

_____

_____

_____

_____

_____

_____

_____

Manifestation is the power you have within. It is the ability to tap into your faith and discernment.

I MANIFESTED THIS SH*T

_____

_____

_____

_____

_____

_____

_____

_____

_____

_____

_____

_____

_____

Manifestation is the power you have within. It is the ability to tap into your faith and discernment.

I MANIFESTED THIS SH*T

_____

_____

_____

_____

_____

_____

_____

_____

_____

_____

_____

_____

_____

_____

Manifestation is the power you have within. It is the ability to tap into your faith and discernment.

I MANIFESTED THIS SH*T

_____

_____

_____

_____

_____

_____

_____

_____

_____

_____

_____

_____

Manifestation is the power you have within. It is the ability to tap into your faith and discernment.

DAY OF THE WEEK: M ☐ T ☐ W ☐ TH ☐ F ☐ S ☐ S ☐

DATE _____   TIME _____

WHERE AM I NOW: HOME ☐ WORK ☐ OTHER _____

SOME OF MY BEST MOMENTS WITH SPIRIT HAPPENED IN THE CAR AND BATHROOM.
WHAT A MIGHTY RELEASE!

I am manifesting a breakthrough and not a breakdown.... (repeat and write)

_____

_____

_____

_____

_____

_____

_____

_____

_____

_____

Manifestation is the power you have within. It is the ability to tap into your faith and discernment.

I MANIFESTED THIS SH*T

_____

_____

_____

_____

_____

_____

_____

_____

_____

_____

_____

_____

_____

Manifestation is the power you have within. It is the ability to tap into your faith and discernment.

I MANIFESTED THIS SH*T

_____

_____

_____

_____

_____

_____

_____

_____

_____

_____

_____

_____

_____

Manifestation is the power you have within. It is the ability to tap into your faith and discernment.

I MANIFESTED THIS SH*T

Manifestation is the power you have within. It is the ability to tap into your faith and discernment.

DAY OF THE WEEK: M ☐ T ☐ W ☐ TH ☐ F ☐ S ☐ S ☐

DATE _____   TIME _____

WHERE AM I NOW: HOME ☐   WORK ☐   OTHER _____

I CRIED TODAY, NOT BECAUSE I AM HURTING, BUT BECAUSE I AM OVERWHELMED OF THE LOVE AND BLESSINGS GIVEN TO ME. THE SPIRIT OF OSHUN IS ON ME.

I am grateful for love, patience and understanding.... (repeat and write)

_____

_____

_____

_____

_____

_____

_____

_____

_____

_____

Manifestation is the power you have within. It is the ability to tap into your faith and discernment.

I MANIFESTED THIS SH*T

_____

_____

_____

_____

_____

_____

_____

_____

_____

_____

_____

_____

_____

Manifestation is the power you have within. It is the ability to tap into your faith and discernment.

I MANIFESTED THIS SH*T

_____

_____

_____

_____

_____

_____

_____

_____

_____

_____

_____

_____

Manifestation is the power you have within. It is the ability to tap into your faith and discernment.

I MANIFESTED THIS SH*T

_____

_____

_____

_____

_____

_____

_____

_____

_____

_____

_____

_____

_____

Manifestation is the power you have within. It is the ability to tap into your faith and discernment.

DAY OF THE WEEK: M ☐ T ☐ W ☐ TH ☐ F ☐ S ☐ S ☐

DATE _____   TIME _____

WHERE AM I NOW: HOME ☐   WORK ☐   OTHER _____

MY STEPS HAVE BEEN ORDERED. MY PRAYERS HAVE BEEN HEARD. I AM WALKING IN AN OVERFLOW.

I deserve abundance, I deserve this overflow.... (repeat and write)

_____

_____

_____

_____

_____

_____

_____

_____

_____

_____

_____

Manifestation is the power you have within. It is the ability to tap into your faith and discernment.

I MANIFESTED THIS SH*T

_____

_____

_____

_____

_____

_____

_____

_____

_____

_____

_____

_____

_____

Manifestation is the power you have within. It is the ability to tap into your faith and discernment.

I MANIFESTED THIS SH*T

_____

_____

_____

_____

_____

_____

_____

_____

_____

_____

_____

_____

_____

_____

Manifestation is the power you have within. It is the ability to tap into your faith and discernment.

I MANIFESTED THIS SH*T

_____

_____

_____

_____

_____

_____

_____

_____

_____

_____

_____

_____

_____

Manifestation is the power you have within. It is the ability to tap into your faith and discernment.

DAY OF THE WEEK: M ☐ T ☐ W ☐ TH ☐ F ☐ S ☐ S ☐

DATE _____   TIME _____

WHERE AM I NOW: HOME ☐   WORK ☐   OTHER _____

I CAME THROUGH MY MOTHER'S WOMB FOR A REASON. THAT WAS MY FIRST PURPOSE IN LIFE. SHE KEPT ME. I'M STILL ALIVE BECAUSE THERE IS MORE.

I am manifesting a purpose filled life.... (repeat and write)

_____

_____

_____

_____

_____

_____

_____

_____

_____

_____

_____

Manifestation is the power you have within. It is the ability to tap into your faith and discernment.

I MANIFESTED THIS SH*T

_____

_____

_____

_____

_____

_____

_____

_____

_____

_____

_____

_____

_____

Manifestation is the power you have within. It is the ability to tap into your faith and discernment.

I MANIFESTED THIS SH*T

_____

_____

_____

_____

_____

_____

_____

_____

_____

_____

_____

_____

Manifestation is the power you have within. It is the ability to tap into your faith and discernment.

I MANIFESTED THIS SH*T

_____

_____

_____

_____

_____

_____

_____

_____

_____

_____

_____

_____

_____

_____

Manifestation is the power you have within. It is the ability to tap into your faith and discernment.

DAY OF THE WEEK: M ☐   T ☐   W ☐   TH ☐   F ☐   S ☐   S ☐

DATE _____   TIME _____

WHERE AM I NOW: HOME ☐   WORK ☐   OTHER _____

I WASN'T BORN WITH A SILVER SPOON IN MY MOUTH. I WAS GIVEN ANCESTRAL TOOLS THAT AIDED ME IN SPIRITUAL WEALTH.

My life is full of prosperity, perseverance, promotions and positivity.... (repeat and write)

_____

_____

_____

_____

_____

_____

_____

_____

_____

_____

Manifestation is the power you have within. It is the ability to tap into your faith and discernment.

I MANIFESTED THIS SH*T

Manifestation is the power you have within. It is the ability to tap into your faith and discernment.

I MANIFESTED THIS SH*T

Manifestation is the power you have within. It is the ability to tap into your faith and discernment.

I MANIFESTED THIS SH*T

_____

_____

_____

_____

_____

_____

_____

_____

_____

_____

_____

Manifestation is the power you have within. It is the ability to tap into your faith and discernment.

DAY OF THE WEEK: M ☐ T ☐ W ☐ TH ☐ F ☐ S ☐ S ☐

DATE _____   TIME _____

WHERE AM I NOW: HOME ☐   WORK ☐   OTHER _____

WHEN YOU ARE TRULY TIRED AND HAVE HAD ENOUGH, YOU WILL MOVE. STAYING IN UNHEALTHY SITUATIONS OF ABUSE, TURMOIL, AND CHAOS WILL LEAVE YOU STAGNATED AND MISERABLE.

I have the courage to improve my current situation.... (repeat and write)

_____

_____

_____

_____

_____

_____

_____

_____

_____

_____

_____

Manifestation is the power you have within. It is the ability to tap into your faith and discernment.

I MANIFESTED THIS SH*T

_____

_____

_____

_____

_____

_____

_____

_____

_____

_____

_____

_____

_____

Manifestation is the power you have within. It is the ability to tap into your faith and discernment.

I MANIFESTED THIS SH*T

_____

_____

_____

_____

_____

_____

_____

_____

_____

_____

_____

_____

_____

Manifestation is the power you have within. It is the ability to tap into your faith and discernment.

I MANIFESTED THIS SH*T

_____

_____

_____

_____

_____

_____

_____

_____

_____

_____

_____

_____

_____

Manifestation is the power you have within. It is the ability to tap into your faith and discernment.

DAY OF THE WEEK: M ☐ T ☐ W ☐ TH ☐ F ☐ S ☐ S ☐

DATE _____   TIME _____

WHERE AM I NOW: HOME ☐   WORK ☐   OTHER _____

NEVER STAY WHERE TOXICITY RESIDES. ENERGY TRAVELS AND SPIRIT SUCKERS EXIST.

PLANT YOUR FEET ON HIGHER GROUND.

I will not match anyone's energy.... (repeat and write)

_____

_____

_____

_____

_____

_____

_____

_____

_____

_____

Manifestation is the power you have within. It is the ability to tap into your faith and discernment.

I MANIFESTED THIS SH*T

_____

_____

_____

_____

_____

_____

_____

_____

_____

_____

_____

_____

Manifestation is the power you have within. It is the ability to tap into your faith and discernment.

I MANIFESTED THIS SH*T

_____

_____

_____

_____

_____

_____

_____

_____

_____

_____

_____

_____

_____

Manifestation is the power you have within. It is the ability to tap into your faith and discernment.

I MANIFESTED THIS SH*T

_____

_____

_____

_____

_____

_____

_____

_____

_____

_____

_____

_____

_____

Manifestation is the power you have within. It is the ability to tap into your faith and discernment.

DAY OF THE WEEK: M ☐ T ☐ W ☐ TH ☐ F ☐ S ☐ S ☐

DATE _____   TIME _____

WHERE AM I NOW: HOME ☐   WORK ☐   OTHER _____

I AM LEARNING TO JUST LET GO AND LET GOD. BE PREPARED AND STILL IN KNOWING THAT ITS ALREADY WORKING OUT FOR MY GOOD.

It is working out for my good, IT WORKED OUT FOR MY GOOD.... (repeat and write)

_____

_____

_____

_____

_____

_____

_____

_____

_____

_____

Manifestation is the power you have within. It is the ability to tap into your faith and discernment.

I MANIFESTED THIS SH*T

Manifestation is the power you have within. It is the ability to tap into your faith and discernment.

I MANIFESTED THIS SH*T

_____

_____

_____

_____

_____

_____

_____

_____

_____

_____

_____

_____

_____

Manifestation is the power you have within. It is the ability to tap into your faith and discernment.

I MANIFESTED THIS SH*T

_____

_____

_____

_____

_____

_____

_____

_____

_____

_____

_____

_____

_____

Manifestation is the power you have within. It is the ability to tap into your faith and discernment.

DAY OF THE WEEK: M ☐ T ☐ W ☐ TH ☐ F ☐ S ☐ S ☐

DATE _____   TIME _____

WHERE AM I NOW: HOME ☐   WORK ☐   OTHER _____

TODAY I SAW A FLOWER ALONE BLOOMING, AND IT MADE ME SMILE. I THEN SAT UNDER A TREE AS THE SUN KISSED MY MELANIN. THE TREES THEN BEGAN TO DANCE FOR ME. I FELT MOTHER EARTH'S AIR CONDITIONER AS THE TREES SHOOK ITS BRANCHES.

THERE IS ALWAYS SOMEONE HIGHER THAN I AM LOOKING OUT FOR ME.... (repeat and write)

_____

_____

_____

_____

_____

_____

_____

_____

_____

_____

Manifestation is the power you have within. It is the ability to tap into your faith and discernment.

I MANIFESTED THIS SH*T

_____

_____

_____

_____

_____

_____

_____

_____

_____

_____

_____

_____

_____

Manifestation is the power you have within. It is the ability to tap into your faith and discernment.

I MANIFESTED THIS SH*T

_____

_____

_____

_____

_____

_____

_____

_____

_____

_____

_____

_____

_____

Manifestation is the power you have within. It is the ability to tap into your faith and discernment.

I MANIFESTED THIS SH*T

_____

_____

_____

_____

_____

_____

_____

_____

_____

_____

_____

_____

Manifestation is the power you have within. It is the ability to tap into your faith and discernment.

DAY OF THE WEEK: M ☐ T ☐ W ☐ TH ☐ F ☐ S ☐ S ☐

DATE _____   TIME _____

WHERE AM I NOW: HOME ☐   WORK ☐   OTHER _____

THERE WILL BE NO LACK THEREOF IN MY FINANCES. ALL BILLS ARE PAID. DEBT IS GONE AWAY. MONEY FLOW IS ATTACHED TO ME.

I am financially blessed.... (repeat and write)

_____

_____

_____

_____

_____

_____

_____

_____

_____

_____

Manifestation is the power you have within. It is the ability to tap into your faith and discernment.

I MANIFESTED THIS SH*T

_____

_____

_____

_____

_____

_____

_____

_____

_____

_____

_____

_____

Manifestation is the power you have within. It is the ability to tap into your faith and discernment.

I MANIFESTED THIS SH*T

_____

_____

_____

_____

_____

_____

_____

_____

_____

_____

_____

_____

_____

Manifestation is the power you have within. It is the ability to tap into your faith and discernment.

I MANIFESTED THIS SH*T

_____

_____

_____

_____

_____

_____

_____

_____

_____

_____

_____

_____

_____

Manifestation is the power you have within. It is the ability to tap into your faith and discernment.

DAY OF THE WEEK: M ☐ T ☐ W ☐ TH ☐ F ☐ S ☐ S ☐

DATE _____   TIME _____

WHERE AM I NOW: HOME ☐   WORK ☐   OTHER _____

THERE IS NOTHING TO COMPARE TO LIFE BEING HARD. YOU HAVE THE POWER TO CHANGE YOUR SITUATION AND GET TO WHERE YOU NEED TO BE. MAKE MOVES OR MOVES WILL BE MADE FOR YOU.

I may not be where I want to be, but I am headed to where I need to be.... (repeat and write)

_____

_____

_____

_____

_____

_____

_____

_____

_____

_____

Manifestation is the power you have within. It is the ability to tap into your faith and discernment.

I MANIFESTED THIS SH*T

_____

_____

_____

_____

_____

_____

_____

_____

_____

_____

_____

_____

Manifestation is the power you have within. It is the ability to tap into your faith and discernment.

I MANIFESTED THIS SH*T

_____

_____

_____

_____

_____

_____

_____

_____

_____

_____

_____

_____

Manifestation is the power you have within. It is the ability to tap into your faith and discernment.

I MANIFESTED THIS SH*T

_____

_____

_____

_____

_____

_____

_____

_____

_____

_____

_____

_____

_____

Manifestation is the power you have within. It is the ability to tap into your faith and discernment.

DAY OF THE WEEK: M ☐ T ☐ W ☐ TH ☐ F ☐ S ☐ S ☐

DATE _____   TIME _____

WHERE AM I NOW: HOME ☐   WORK ☐   OTHER _____

GET OUT THERE AND SHOW THE WORLD WHAT YOU ARE MADE OF. DO NOT LET ANY OF YOUR GIFTS PERISH. THERE ARE PEOPLE IN THE CEMETERIES THAT WISH THEY HAD ANOTHER CHANCE. YOUR GIFTS WILL MAKE ROOM FOR YOUR INCREASE.

I will take this chance to use my gifts.... (repeat and write)

_____

_____

_____

_____

_____

_____

_____

_____

_____

_____

Manifestation is the power you have within. It is the ability to tap into your faith and discernment.

I MANIFESTED THIS SH*T

Manifestation is the power you have within. It is the ability to tap into your faith and discernment.

I MANIFESTED THIS SH*T

_____

_____

_____

_____

_____

_____

_____

_____

_____

_____

_____

_____

_____

Manifestation is the power you have within. It is the ability to tap into your faith and discernment.

I MANIFESTED THIS SH*T

_____

_____

_____

_____

_____

_____

_____

_____

_____

_____

_____

_____

_____

Manifestation is the power you have within. It is the ability to tap into your faith and discernment.

DAY OF THE WEEK: M ☐ T ☐ W ☐ TH ☐ F ☐ S ☐ S ☐

DATE _____   TIME _____

WHERE AM I NOW: HOME ☐   WORK ☐   OTHER _____

TALKED ABOUT, LAUGHED AT AND BETRAYED; BUT ONE THING FOR CERTAIN, MY UNIQUE SELF HAS CAPTIVATED THE ATTENTION OF THOSE THAT MIMIC ME.

I am favored by the Almighty, my cup is filled with victory everywhere.... (repeat and write)

_____

_____

_____

_____

_____

_____

_____

_____

_____

_____

Manifestation is the power you have within. It is the ability to tap into your faith and discernment.

I MANIFESTED THIS SH*T

_____

_____

_____

_____

_____

_____

_____

_____

_____

_____

_____

_____

_____

Manifestation is the power you have within. It is the ability to tap into your faith and discernment.

I MANIFESTED THIS SH*T

_____

_____

_____

_____

_____

_____

_____

_____

_____

_____

_____

_____

Manifestation is the power you have within. It is the ability to tap into your faith and discernment.

I MANIFESTED THIS SH*T

Manifestation is the power you have within. It is the ability to tap into your faith and discernment.

DAY OF THE WEEK: M ☐ T ☐ W ☐ TH ☐ F ☐ S ☐ S ☐

DATE _____   TIME _____

WHERE AM I NOW: HOME ☐   WORK ☐   OTHER _____

I AM ALWAYS MY TRUE DIVINE SELF, UNIQUELY MADE, OFTEN IMITATED, NEVER DUPLICATED.

I am just amazing.... (repeat and write)

_____

_____

_____

_____

_____

_____

_____

_____

_____

_____

_____

Manifestation is the power you have within. It is the ability to tap into your faith and discernment.

I MANIFESTED THIS SH*T

Manifestation is the power you have within. It is the ability to tap into your faith and discernment.

I MANIFESTED THIS SH*T

Manifestation is the power you have within. It is the ability to tap into your faith and discernment.

I MANIFESTED THIS SH*T

Manifestation is the power you have within. It is the ability to tap into your faith and discernment.

DAY OF THE WEEK: M ☐ T ☐ W ☐ TH ☐ F ☐ S ☐ S ☐

DATE _____   TIME _____

WHERE AM I NOW: HOME ☐   WORK ☐   OTHER _____

DESPITE THAT OTHER VOICE TELLING YOU, YOU CAN'T...DO IT ANYWAY. WIN, LOSE OR DRAW, DO ME A FAVOR DON'T DIE NOT TRYING.

I can and I will accomplish my goals.... (repeat and write)

_____

_____

_____

_____

_____

_____

_____

_____

_____

_____

Manifestation is the power you have within. It is the ability to tap into your faith and discernment.

I MANIFESTED THIS SH*T

_____

_____

_____

_____

_____

_____

_____

_____

_____

_____

_____

_____

_____

Manifestation is the power you have within. It is the ability to tap into your faith and discernment.

I MANIFESTED THIS SH*T

_____

_____

_____

_____

_____

_____

_____

_____

_____

_____

_____

_____

_____

Manifestation is the power you have within. It is the ability to tap into your faith and discernment.

I MANIFESTED THIS SH*T

_____

_____

_____

_____

_____

_____

_____

_____

_____

_____

_____

_____

_____

_____

Manifestation is the power you have within. It is the ability to tap into your faith and discernment.

DAY OF THE WEEK: M ☐   T ☐   W ☐ TH ☐   F ☐   S ☐   S ☐

DATE _____   TIME _____

WHERE AM I NOW: HOME ☐   WORK ☐   OTHER _____

UNHEALED PEOPLE CREATE UNHEALED SITUATIONS, AND IT JUST GOES ON AND ON AND ON AND ON.

I am healed from the torment of unhealed people.... (repeat and write)

_____

_____

_____

_____

_____

_____

_____

_____

_____

_____

_____

Manifestation is the power you have within. It is the ability to tap into your faith and discernment.

I MANIFESTED THIS SH*T

Manifestation is the power you have within. It is the ability to tap into your faith and discernment.

I MANIFESTED THIS SH*T

_____

_____

_____

_____

_____

_____

_____

_____

_____

_____

_____

_____

_____

_____

Manifestation is the power you have within. It is the ability to tap into your faith and discernment.

I MANIFESTED THIS SH*T

Manifestation is the power you have within. It is the ability to tap into your faith and discernment.